EcoWorks

HOW A SOLAR-POWERED HOME WORKS

Robyn Hardyman

W
FRANKLIN WATTS
LONDON • SYDNEY

First published in 2015 by Franklin Watts
338 Euston Road
London NW1 3BH

Franklin Watts Australia
Level 17/207 Kent Street
Sydney, NSW 2000

Produced by Calcium

A CIP catalogue record for this book is available from the British Library.

ISBN 978 1 4451 3905 0

Dewey classification: 720.4'724

Printed in China

Franklin Watts is a division of Hachette Children's Books, an Hachette UK company
www.hachette.co.uk

Acknowledgements:
The publisher would like to thank the following for permission to reproduce photographs: Cover: Shutterstock: Elena Elisseeva. Inside: Dreamstime: Airwolf01 24, Antoniosena 19, Erikreis 6, Monkeybusinessimages 5b, 8, Photosell247 20, David Watmough 21b; Energy for Opportunity: 29t; Shutterstock: Anweber 1, 16, Mile Atanasov 9, Bennyartist 14, Rob Byron 13, M. Cornelius 11, Elena Elisseeva 15, Esbobeldijk 18, Paul Fleet 21t, Igor Kovalchuk 5t, lladyjane 7, Daleen Loest 26, Luiggi33 10, Neijia 2–3, NorGal 12, Ollirg 23, Joshua Resnick 22, YuriyZhuravov 4; Solar Roadways: 28–29; Wikipedia: CalderOliver 17t, Peellden 27, S-kei 17b, Solúcar 25.

Every attempt has been made to clear copyright. Should there be any inadvertent omission please apply to the publisher for rectification.

Contents

Energy from the sun

The sun is a star: a huge burning ball of gases in space. It is so enormous, a million Earths would fit inside it. This flaming giant produces a massive amount of energy. Scientists have found ways to use some of this energy to meet our need for power.

Plants use the light of the sun to make food so they can grow.

Using the sun

The sun lights our world and gives us heat. This light and heat make all life on Earth possible. Plants make food from sunlight, and animals eat plants. For thousands of years, people have been using the sun's light and heat. We have grown food crops in sunlight and concentrated the sun's rays to light fires. Now we are finding even better ways to harness this power.

4

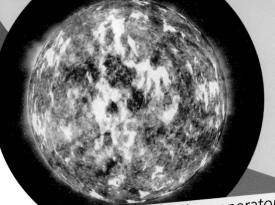

Solar power up close

In every minute, enough energy from the sun reaches the Earth to meet the whole world's energy needs for a year. What is more, it takes that energy just eight minutes to travel the 150 million kilometres to get here!

The sun is a massive generator of energy.

Why do we need solar power?

We use energy every day, for hundreds of tasks, from switching on the lights to watching TV. Mostly this energy is in the form of electricity that is supplied by cables from a power station. Power stations can make electricity in different ways. Most of our electricity is made by burning huge quantities of coal, oil and gas. These are called fossil fuels. They took millions of years to form underground. There is a limited amount of them, and we cannot make more. Coal, oil and gas are not sustainable. Burning them creates harmful pollution as well.

Our demand for energy is increasing all the time as the population grows. We need to find cleaner, more sustainable sources of energy, such as the wind, the waves – and solar power from the sun.

We use electricity all the time at home, at school and at work.

Using solar power

Solar power is created using the energy from the sun. This energy comes in two forms: heat and light. We can use both of these to meet our increasing need for energy in our homes. In the future, the way we design and build our homes will be affected by how we power them.

Passive solar power

Have you noticed how sunlight streaming through a window can make your home feel warmer, even on a cold day? That is passive solar power in action. Our homes can be designed to make the best use of both the heat and the light of the sun. We can build our homes to get the most sunlight through the windows.

The sun lights and warms our homes during the day.

Smart design

In the northern hemisphere, new buildings need to face south – or north in the southern hemisphere. We can also use good insulation to trap the heat of the sun. This means building walls and roofs with materials that stop heat escaping.

Cool in summer

In summer, too much sunshine streaming in through large windows may make rooms overheat. Buildings can be designed with extended roofs to shade large windows and keep everyone comfortable.

In a garden, we trap the heat of the sun in a greenhouse to help our food and flower plants grow.

Passive solar power up close

People in ancient times understood all about passive solar power. The ancient Greeks built whole cities of houses that were positioned to be warmed by the sun in winter, while blocking its heat in summer. The ancient Romans were the first to put glass in windows. They had learned that in winter this made rooms warmer as well as brighter.

Solar thermal power

Along with collecting passive solar energy, we can also use energy from the sun to power our buildings and machinery. Solar thermal power is created using the heat of the sun. Solar thermal power is used to heat water. In an average home in the developed world, a person uses around 120 litres of hot water every day, for showers, baths, laundry or washing dishes. Instead of using gas or electricity to heat the water, we can use the sun!

Using the sun to power your dishwasher could save you up to £50 per year and will also help the environment.

How it works

A solar water heater heats up household water before it enters the home's conventional gas or electric water heater. The sun's heat is collected by a device on the roof of a building, called a collector. Flat plate collectors are the most common type. Collectors are installed on a slope or roof on the side of the building that receives the most sunshine. They heat water that is then pumped to a storage tank.

When you turn on the tap, heated water from the storage tank flows into the conventional water heater. If it is hot enough, it comes out as it is. If not, the gas or electric heater makes it hotter.

Where it works

Solar water heaters heat water only when the sun is shining on them. This means that they are ideal for sunny places, such as Australia, where they can provide almost all of a household's hot water. They are less suitable for cloudy locations, such as much of northern Europe.

This evacuated tube collector is positioned to face south, to absorb the maximum amount of heat from the sun.

ECO FACT

Heating water

The most up-to-date type of collector is an evacuated tube collector. It heats water effectively. It consists of a series of metal pipes containing a liquid that heats up. Each pipe is enclosed in a double-walled glass tube, painted black to absorb heat. The air between the walls of the glass tube is removed (or evacuated), creating a vacuum. This works just like a vacuum flask, keeping in the heat.

Solar thermal power outdoors

Solar thermal power can be used for many things besides giving us hot showers at home. Outdoors, it can be used to heat swimming pools, so we can enjoy swimming all year round. Another use is even more vital – cooking food!

Hot and sunny

Using the power of the sun to heat the water in an outdoor pool makes good sense. Outdoor pools are mostly located in warm, sunny places, where there is plenty of solar energy. Simple solar collectors are installed on a sloping roof near the pool, usually the roof of the pool house. They can easily heat the water to the typical pool temperature of 24–30 °C.

Pool water is pumped through solar collectors on the pool-house roof to heat the water to a comfortable temperature.

Cooking with the sun

Solar cooking is a simple and safe way to cook food. It uses no electricity or fire. For the millions of people around the world who do not have access to electricity, solar cooking is an important breakthrough. Traditional cooking methods, which involve fires fuelled by wood or dung, can be bad for health and the environment. Solar ovens enable people to cook cleanly and for free. Solar ovens can also be used to boil drinking water to make it safe.

Solar ovens are an inventive way to use the sun's heat in developing countries. They are now becoming popular in developed countries, too, where people are using solar ovens to cook outdoors during the summer.

ECO FACT

How a solar oven works

A simple solar oven is a box surrounded by reflective panels. These direct the sunlight onto the food, which is placed inside, in a closed cooking pot. The food is cut into small pieces to help it cook quicker. The oven is positioned in full sunlight, and cooking takes place over several hours. Although this is much slower than a fuel-based oven, the food can be left unattended. Food cooks fastest during the hottest part of the day.

Electricity from sunlight

We have been using the heat of the sun for all of human history. But in the past 50 years, there has been a big breakthrough – we have found out how to use the sun's energy to make electricity!

This calculator is powered by tiny photovoltaic panels.

Solar panels

Electricity powers many of the machines we use. Making electricity directly from sunlight is sustainable, because the energy supply will never run out. Also, solar power creates no pollution. Sunlight is turned into electricity using solar panels, in a process called photovoltaics, or PV. Small PV panels have been used to power devices such as calculators and clocks for decades. To make enough electricity to power our homes, we need bigger and better systems.

This house is a research project. It is powered entirely by solar power, with PV panels and a solar water heater on the roof.

How much electricity?

Electricity is measured in watts. A kilowatt (KW) is 1,000 watts, a megawatt (MW) is 1 million watts. We measure the electricity used over time in kilowatt-hours or megawatt-hours. The average United Kingdom household uses around 4,600 kilowatt-hours of electricity per year.

Some energy-efficient homes, however, use around 2,000 kilowatt-hours of electricity per year. In a sunny climate, a 2 kilowatt PV system can produce 3,600 kilowatt-hours of electricity per year. Australians use more megawatt hours than most other countries in the world.

ECO FACT

Discovering solar electricity

Solar electricity may be a twenty-first century energy, but it was discovered by a French physicist, Edmond Becquerel, nearly two centuries ago. In 1839, he found that some materials generate very small amounts of electricity when they are exposed to sunlight. More than a century later, in 1954, Bell Laboratories in the United States developed a photovoltaic panel that consumers could use.

How solar cells work

A photovoltaic solar panel is made up of a number of photovoltaic cells joined together. It is in each of these cells that the electricity is made.

A solar cell

Solar cells are made of several layers that are joined together. The top layer is glass, for protection. The next is a dark layer to keep the sunlight from reflecting off the glass. Under that are two thin wafers made of silicon and metal wires. The wafers are made by heating the silicon to a very high temperature. Chemicals are added to it that make particles in the silicon, called electrons, less tightly bonded to each other. When sunlight hits the silicon wafers, the electrons absorb some of the sun's energy. This makes them start to move, and they flow along the metal wires. This movement of electrons is an electric current, or electricity.

Some solar panels, such as these PV cells, are more efficient than others (see opposite).

Photovoltaic panels

Photovoltaic cells are joined together to make modules. These modules are then combined to make PV panels. The panels are installed on the roof of a building. The number of panels used depends on how much power is going to be needed in the building. The panels must be installed so that they get as much sunlight as possible. This means putting them on a roof, tilted up at an angle and facing in the direction that will catch the most sunshine.

PV panels are installed to catch the maximum amount of sunshine.

Too hot?

Excessive heat is not good for solar panels – it makes them perform less well. A panel will produce more electricity on a sunny, cold day (especially if snow is reflecting the sunlight), than on a hot, clear day.

Solar cells up close

The most efficient PV modules, the ones that convert more of the sun's energy into electricity, are modules with polka dots or octagons. They are usually very dark, or black. The less efficient ones are pure blue, but are cheaper to produce.

15

The solar system

The solar panel creates electricity for your home, but how does it actually connect to your power supply? First, the electricity must be made safe for using in the home. It must also be stored, so that it can be used at times when the panels are not able to generate electricity.

Using your solar power

The PV panels on the roof can be connected to a battery, which stores the electricity generated by the solar system. Your house can also be connected to the grid.

The grid is a country's main utility network. The grid will supply power if you have not generated enough from your solar panels. For example, at times of the year when there is less sunshine, people can use electricity from the grid instead of their solar power systems.

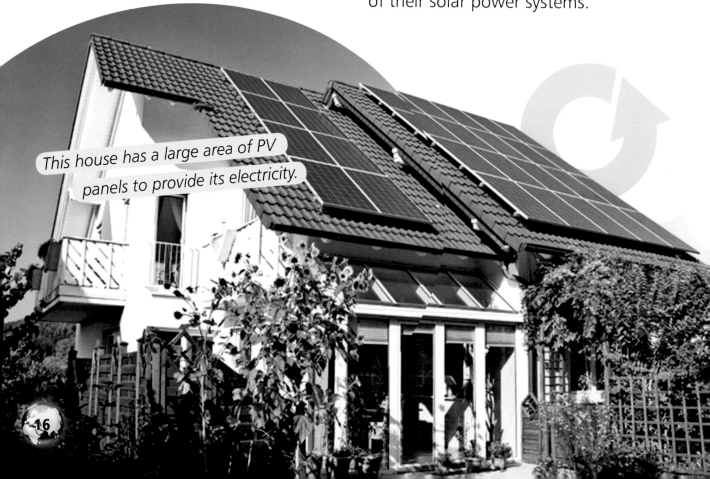

This house has a large area of PV panels to provide its electricity.

Make money from solar power

If your solar panels are generating more electricity than you need, you can give the excess back to the utility company, which will pay you for it. However, the rate, or tariff, you get is less than the utility company itself charges for electricity.

Many solar power systems also allow people to have a home electricity meter that runs backwards as well as forwards! This happens when power is being put back into the grid rather than taken out. The process is called net metering.

PV panels can be installed on blocks of flats, too.

Electricity up close

The electricity produced by PV panels is direct current (DC). However, we need alternating current (AC) electricity to power our homes because it is safer than DC. In the solar power system, the electricity is converted from DC to AC in a device called an inverter. The electricity is then directed to the fuse box, where it is channelled to power different areas of the house, such as lights and plug sockets.

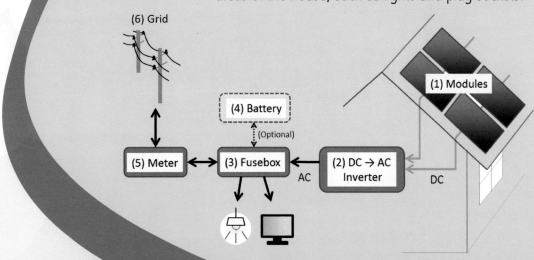

(6) Grid

(4) Battery

(Optional)

(5) Meter ⟷ (3) Fusebox ← AC ← (2) DC → AC Inverter ← DC ← (1) Modules

A regular supply

You have set up your solar panels on the roof, and on a sunny day they make a lot of electricity. But what happens when the sun is not shining? It is vital to have a regular power supply you can rely on.

Sunshine or cloud?

PV panels can only produce electricity when the sun is shining on them. They are most effective at midday, in full sun. When the sun is low in the sky, at the beginning and end of the day, or in winter, less sunlight falls on them and they are less effective. In the United Kingdom there are, on average, 4 hours of usable sunshine per day in summer and 1 hour in winter. Western Australia receives more than 6 hours of usable sunshine per day all year round.

On a cloudy day, these PV panels will make less electricity than in full sunshine.

Reducing consumption

The number of PV panels a home needs depends on how much power is used, and on the local climate. To generate 2 kilowatts of power you need around 16 square metres of solar panels, which is a big area. By reducing your electricity consumption, you will need fewer panels. This can be done through insulation, using energy-efficient appliances and by turning things off!

On a flat roof, PV panels can be angled to get the most sunlight possible.

Storing power

So how can your solar-powered home keep going when it is cloudy or during the night? In bright sunlight, the panels may have made more electricity than your home needs. This excess electricity is stored in the battery, ready for watching TV, washing dishes or simply lighting the home at night.

Solar electricity outside

As well as providing electricity for appliances and lighting inside your home, the sun can power many outdoor devices.

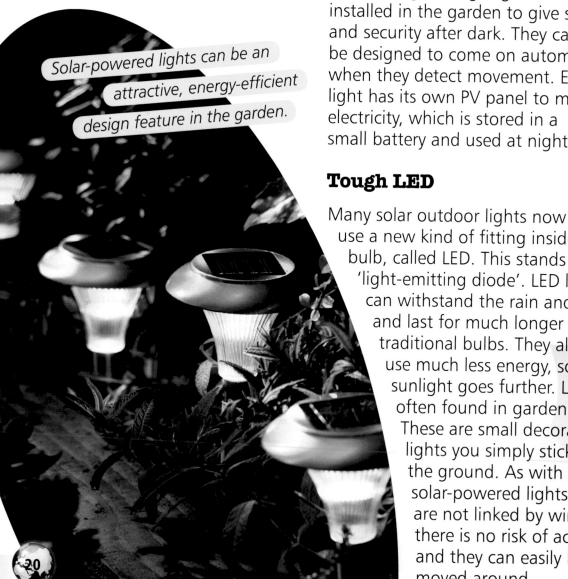

Solar-powered lights can be an attractive, energy-efficient design feature in the garden.

Lights at night

Solar-powered lights are great for places where it can be difficult to run electric cables. They are powered by the sun during the day so they can shine at night. Large lights can be installed in the garden to give safety and security after dark. They can even be designed to come on automatically when they detect movement. Each light has its own PV panel to make electricity, which is stored in a small battery and used at night.

Tough LED

Many solar outdoor lights now use a new kind of fitting inside the bulb, called LED. This stands for 'light-emitting diode'. LED lights can withstand the rain and sun, and last for much longer than traditional bulbs. They also use much less energy, so your sunlight goes further. LEDs are often found in garden lights. These are small decorative lights you simply stick in the ground. As with all solar-powered lights, they are not linked by wires, so there is no risk of accidents and they can easily be moved around.

This satellite is powered by hundreds of PV panels.

The ultimate outdoors

Solar panels are used somewhere else outdoors – way out in space! The satellites that travel around Earth to create our communication systems are covered in many PV panels. That is what powers them.

ECO FACT

This roadside sign is powered by PV cells.

Sending a message

Next time you are on the motorway, look out for the big flashing signs with messages for motorists. Some are operated by solar power – you will see they have solar panels above them, and a battery to store the electricity, so that they work 24 hours a day. Solar-powered signs can be found closer to home, too. You may see them at junctions or on the roadside. There are even solar-powered streetlights and parking meters.

The limitations of solar power

Solar power has many advantages. We will never run out of power from the sun and creating electricity from it does not produce any pollution. It does have a few disadvantages, however. These are the reasons why solar power has not taken over from burning fossil fuels.

A PV cell will create little energy when the weather is cloudy and none at all at night.

More power, please

Solar panels can convert only around one-fifth of the energy in sunlight into electricity. The rest is wasted. This is not very efficient. Coal-fired power stations convert around one-third of the coal's energy into electricity. Scientists are working hard to improve solar power's efficiency, which has so far limited the use of this new technology.

The costs up close

A major factor affecting the popularity of solar power is the cost. Solar panels are expensive to make, and to install. For the individual, using a solar-power system will pay for itself in the long-term by greatly reducing electricity bills and maintenance costs. Making electricity with solar power costs a lot more than burning coal and gas, but if you factor in the cost of using up all our fossil fuels, and the damage to the environment through climate change, it does not seem so expensive.

Old habits

They say 'old habits die hard', and it is true that people often hesitate before they change something that is already working fine. Many people are resistant to changing the way they use energy.

Making the change

We already have many power stations fired by coal and gas, and plenty of electricity from the grid, so why switch? Maybe it will be your generation that will lead the way in making solar power more affordable and widely used worldwide.

Solar power is expensive to install, but it saves users money in the long term as the sunlight is free.

Solar power for everyone

Solar power is not just for individual homes and businesses. It can be generated in solar power stations and distributed to everyone. Just like solar power options in your home, there are thermal and photovoltaic solar power stations, too.

All solar power stations cover huge areas of land. This one uses PV panels.

Photovoltaic power stations

PV power stations use thousands of panels to create electricity, which is then connected to the grid.

The Greenough River Solar Farm in western Australia is one of the country's biggest power stations. In Wiltshire in the United Kingdom, Westmill Solar is the biggest community-owned solar project.

Solar thermal power

The world's first commercial solar thermal power station, called Solucar, opened in Spain in 2007. In the countryside, two massive towers are surrounded by a field of more than 600 huge mirrors. Each mirror reflects the sunlight and focuses it on one place at the top of the tower.

This tower at Solucar is 115 metres tall. The hundreds of angled mirrors track the sun as it moves across the sky.

The intense heat created by the reflected light heats up water, which produces steam. This steam runs turbines, or huge engines, which generate power. As a result, enough electricity is produced to power up to 10,000 homes in the area.

Even bigger

A much bigger solar power station has started operating in California, United States, in the Mojave Desert. The Ivanpah Solar Electric Generating System includes three towers and more than 170,000 mirrors. It can produce around the same amount of electricity as one medium-sized fossil fuel power plant.

ECO FACT

The power of mirrors

Solar thermal power stations use hundreds, sometimes thousands, of curved mirrors. These concentrate the sun's rays to heat a special liquid in pipes. The heat in this liquid then heats water and creates steam, to run a turbine, which creates usable energy. The mirrors are called 'parabolic troughs'.

25

Where in the world?

Some countries have taken up solar power more than others. The most solar-savvy countries are not always the sunniest, and other factors affect the development of this eco-friendly energy.

Huge growth

The solar industry is growing fast worldwide. Germany and China lead the world in the production of PV panels. More than 1 million homes in Australia – one-tenth of the total – now have solar panels. New solar power plants will add even more capacity in future years.

The developing world

In countries where the supply of electricity is poor, solar power can make a huge difference. India has large power stations in development. In Africa, there are plans for small solar systems to bring power to areas where there is no electricity grid.

In many African countries, solar power is bringing electricity to rural areas for the first time.

Making solar pay

One of the drawbacks of solar power is the high cost of getting started. In some countries, people have been given financial help to 'go solar'. Schemes contribute towards the start-up costs or pay customers for any electricity they put back into the grid.

The government in Germany has pledged to get 25 per cent of all its electricity from solar power by 2050. Germany tops the list of solar producers worldwide. In order to meet a European Union target, the United Kingdom has to find 15 per cent of its energy needs from renewable sources, including solar power, by 2020.

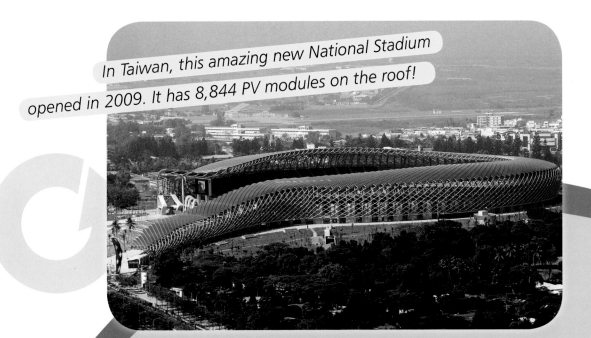

In Taiwan, this amazing new National Stadium opened in 2009. It has 8,844 PV modules on the roof!

Global solar power up close

This table shows the top ten producers of PV solar power in 2013. Spain is the global leader in solar thermal power, producing 65 per cent of the world's total capacity.

Producers of PV solar power in 2013

Country	Megawatts produced
Germany	32,400
Italy	16,400
China	8,300
United States	7,800
Japan	6,900
Spain	5,200
France	4,000
Belgium	2,700
Australia	2,700
Czech Republic	2,100

Solar-powered future

Solar power's share of the world's energy output is small but growing fast. New technology is making PV panels more efficient. As they become more popular, the costs are really coming down, too. People are coming up with new ideas, too, for ways to use solar power.

New technology

It is currently estimated that for an initial investment of £7,000 to install a solar panel system in the average UK home, the owner can expect to save £785 per year on their energy bills. This makes solar power an attractive choice for homes, and for businesses, too.

The cost of installing solar panels is also falling, making the energy system more affordable for many people. Since 2008, the price of silicon PV panels in the United Kingdom has dropped by 50 per cent. A new kind of PV panel, called thin-film PV, is even cheaper to make. It may be less efficient than silicon cells, but it is perfect for large-scale projects, such as PV power stations.

New ideas

People everywhere are developing amazing ideas for using solar power. How about see-through solar

The future will bring many creative new uses for solar power, such as this US solar-panel road.

panels to use as windows? Or roads made of solar panels that could charge your electric car as you drive? Heating elements in streets, and on pavements, could melt ice and snow. These ideas are all being explored.

New opportunities

Countries in the developing world need access to electricity to allow them to grow, and to improve the quality of people's lives. Solar power can make a huge difference. Building solar power plants in sunny locations can bring power to large areas. On a smaller scale, solar panels on individual buildings can bring power to villages, for agricultural use or for essential health services.

A project called Energy For Opportunity is installing solar systems in West Africa to bring electricity to people 'off-grid'.

ECO FACT

Solar future

A new kind of thin-film PV cell is being developed. It is made from copper, zinc and tin, which are cheaper than the indium and gallium used in existing thin-film cells. They are more efficient, too. These cells can simply be printed onto a surface, giving them even more possible uses.

Glossary

alternating current (AC) the type of electricity used to power homes and businesses

battery a device for collecting and storing electricity

collector the part of a solar thermal system that collects the heat in sunshine

direct current (DC) the type of electricity produced by a solar PV panel, which is then converted into alternating current (AC) by an inverter

electrons very small particles found in all matter

evacuated tube collector a solar energy collector that uses a series of vacuum tubes to absorb the sunlight

flat plate collector a solar energy collector that uses a network of tubes under a flat glass surface to absorb the sunlight

fossil fuels coal, oil and natural gas

fusebox the place in a home from where the electricity is wired to all rooms

grid the network that distributes electricity from power stations to consumers

hemisphere half of Earth – there are two hemispheres: a northern hemisphere and a southern hemisphere

insulation a covering or protection that prevents heat being lost from a building

inverter the device in a PV solar system that converts DC electricity to AC electricity for safe use

net metering a system where a home electricity meter can run backwards once that home is putting solar power back into the grid instead of taking power from it

passive solar heating when the heat of the sun naturally warms a building by shining on it or through windows

photovoltaic cell the smallest part of a solar power system, where the sunlight is converted to electricity

photovoltaics (PV) the process of creating electricity from the light of the sun

pollution dirt or harmful substances

silicon a substance derived from sand that is used to make one kind of PV cell

solar thermal power power created using the heat of the sun

sustainable a source that will never run out, such as the sun or wind

thin-film PV a type of photovoltaic cell made using substances other than silicon

turbine an engine driven by a flow of steam to create energy

utility a company that produces, and sometimes also distributes, electricity to consumers

vacuum a space with no air in it

watt the unit of measurement for electricity

For more information

Books

Let's Discuss Energy Resources: Solar Power, Richard and Louise Spilsbury, Wayland

Solar Power: Energy for Free? (World Energy Issues), Jim Pipe, Franklin Watts

Solar Power (Energy for Today), Tea Benduhn, Gareth Stevens Publishing

Solar Power (Tales of Invention), Chris Oxlade, Raintree

The Kids' Solar Energy Book, Tilly Spetgang and Malcolm Wells, Imagine Publishing

Websites

Find out how many solar panels it takes to heat a home at:
**www.energymatters.com.au/education/
solar-kids-teens.php**

Enter the 'energy info zone' to watch videos on different kinds of energy, including solar power, at:
www.sciencemuseum.org.uk/on-line/energy/site/EIZinfogr.asp

Discover the amazing story of PV cells at:
http://schoolgen.co.nz/students/solar-energy-factsheets

Note to parents and teachers
Every effort has been made by the Publisher to ensure that these websites contain no inappropriate or offensive material. However, because of the nature of the Internet, it is impossible to guarantee that the contents of these sites will not be altered. We strongly advise that Internet access is supervised by a responsible adult.

Index